CAMP OUT!

THE ESSENTIAL COOKBOOK TO BRING CIVILIZATION TO THE WILD!

First published in 2013
LOVE FOOD is an imprint of Parragon Books Ltd

Parragon
Chartist House
15–17 Trim Street
Bath, BA1 1HA, UK

LOVE FOOD and the accompanying heart device is a registered trademark of Parragon Books Ltd in Australia, the UK, USA, India, and the EU.

www.parragon.com/lovefood

ISBN: 978-1-4723-0286-1

Printed in China

Notes for the Reader
This book uses standard kitchen measuring spoons and cups. All spoon and cup measurements are level unless otherwise indicated. Unless otherwise stated, milk is assumed to be whole, butter is assumed to be salted, eggs are large, individual vegetables are medium, and pepper is freshly ground black pepper. Unless otherwise stated, all root vegetables should be washed and peeled before using.

For the best results, use a meat thermometer when cooking meat and poultry—check the latest USDA government guidelines for current advice.

Garnishes and serving suggestions are optional and not necessarily included in the recipe ingredients or method. The times given are only an approximate guide. Preparation times differ according to the techniques used by different people and the cooking times may also vary from those given.

Recipes using raw or very lightly cooked eggs should be avoided by infants, the elderly, pregnant women, and people with weakened immune systems. Pregnant and breast-feeding women are advised to avoid eating peanuts and peanut products. People with nut allergies should be aware that some of the prepared ingredients used in the recipes in this book may contain nuts. Always check the packaging before use.

Vegetarians should be aware that some of the prepared ingredients used in the recipes in this book may contain animal products. Always check the package before use.

CONTENTS

PLUS!
TIPS ON HOW TO BEAT BAD WEATHER BLUES
PAGE 28

INTRODUCTION

Whether you go on vacation by the beach, head to a camping area to enjoy a wilderness experience, or go away to a weekend festival, camping is a quick, inexpensive getaway for the summer months. Shrug off the stresses of modern life: turn off your phone, put down the laptop, unplug the TV—and embrace evenings under the stars. Whether you are camping or "glamping," stripped back to basics, camping is simply good for the soul!

Obviously, before embarking upon a vacation under canvas, you'll need to stock up on some basic equipment. Whatever your budget, you can find all the essentials at specialty outdoor stores or online. Naturally, the tent will be your biggest purchase—if you're planning an extended trip (and you aren't backpacking), consider a tent that's large enough to stand up in, with space to eat in if the weather is bad. For the ultimate camping luxury, invest in an additional "bedroom"—it's invaluable storage space. Other key items are the bedding (an air bed, roll mat, or even both

will be essential to a good night's sleep), plus sleeping bags and cooking equipment. If you can sleep and eat in comfort, anything else will be a bonus.

There's a huge range of nifty cooking equipment available, from the humble gas burner, to the disposable barbecue, to top of the range gas-powered grills, but you should invest in an item that's suitable for your trip. Consider how many you will be cooking for, and the kinds of food you're intending to eat.

Even if you will have access to stores, try planning your meals before you go away, and make sure you discuss food ideas with everyone who's involved in the camping trip (this will prevent a lot of arguing later on). Work out all the meals in advance so all that's needed are clever staple ingredients combined with some fresh produce—and if you have access to a freezer, maybe some frozen items taken from home. All that's left is to cook, eat, and enjoy!

BREAKFAST BAGELS

Serves: 4

Prep: 5 mins

Cook: 5 mins

4 eggs

1 tablespoon
sunflower oil

4 multiseeded bagels

8 slices American
cheese

4 slices ham

salt and pepper,
to taste

1. Lightly beat the eggs with 1 tablespoon of water and season with salt and pepper. Heat the oil in a skillet over a campfire, stove, or barbecue. Pour in the eggs and cook, stirring lightly, until set. Remove the omelet from the heat and cut into four pieces.

2. Cut the bagels in half and toast lightly. Place a slice of cheese on the bottom half of each bagel, then top with a piece of omelet and a slice of ham.

3. Top with another slice of cheese and add the top half of the bagel. Serve immediately.

Swap the ham for strips of cooked bacon and the omelet for fried eggs to create a bacon and egg bagel

GREEK YOGURT
(with honey, nuts & blueberries)

Serves: 4

Prep: 5 mins

Cook: 5 mins

3 tablespoons honey

1 cup mixed
unsalted nuts

1½ cups Greek yogurt

1½ cups fresh
blueberries

1 Gently heat the honey in a small saucepan over a campfire, stove, or barbecue. Add the nuts and stir until they are well coated. Remove from the heat and let cool slightly.

2 To serve, divide the yogurt among four bowls, then spoon the nut mixture and blueberries over the yogurt.

Start your day with a health-boosting combo of Greek yogurt, nuts, and blueberries—without sugar or sweeteners!

CHICKEN NOODLE SOUP

 Serves: 4–6

Prep: 10 mins

Cook: 30–35 mins

- - - - - - - - - - - - - - - - - - -

2 skinless chicken breasts

5 cups water or chicken stock

3 carrots, cut into ¼-inch-thick slices

4 ounces dried vermicelli (or other small noodles)

salt and pepper, to taste

1 Place the chicken breasts in a large saucepan, add the water, and bring to a simmer over a campfire, stove, or barbecue. Cook for 25–30 minutes, or until the chicken is cooked through. Skim any froth from the surface, if necessary. Remove the chicken from the stock and wrap in aluminum foil to keep warm.

2 Continue to simmer the stock, add the carrots and vermicelli, and cook for 4–5 minutes, or until the noodles are tender.

3 Thinly slice the chicken breasts and place in bowls.

4 Season the soup with salt and pepper and pour it over the chicken. Serve immediately.

Make a batch of soup in the morning and transfer to a flask for on-the-go eating during the day.

BUTTERFLIED WHOLE CHICKEN
(with lemon-oregano butter)

 Serves: 4–6

Prep: 15 mins

Cook: 30–40 mins

1 whole chicken, weighing 3½ pounds

Lemon-oregano butter

1 stick unsalted butter, at room temperature

3 garlic cloves, finely chopped

1 tablespoon chopped fresh oregano

1 teaspoon salt

½ teaspoon pepper

zest and juice of 1 lemon

1 Preheat a grill rack over a campfire or barbecue.

2 To make the lemon-oregano butter, put all the ingredients into a small bowl and mix with a fork until well combined.

3 To butterfly the chicken, use kitchen scissors to cut along both sides of the backbone and remove it. Next, remove the breastbone, which runs down the middle of the breast, and trim off any excess skin and fat.

4 Slide your fingers gently under the skin of the breast and legs to separate it from the meat. Spread 2–3 tablespoons of the butter mixture under the skin. Spread about 1 tablespoon over the outside.

5 Place the chicken on the preheated rack, breast side up, and cook over medium heat for 10 minutes. Baste with more of the butter mixture, turn the chicken breast side down, and continue to cook, turning and basting every 10 minutes, for a total cooking time of 30–40 minutes, or until the chicken is tender and the juices run clear when the tip of a sharp knife is inserted into the thickest part of the meat. Carve and serve immediately.

Prepare the chicken at home, and refrigerate until ready to cook. Or buy a grill-ready butterflied chicken and skip step 3.

BARBECUED CHICKEN WINGS

Serves: 4

Prep: 5 mins

Cook: 20–25 mins

¼ cup tomato paste

2 tablespoons
Worcestershire sauce

1 garlic clove, crushed

1 tablespoon honey

16 chicken wings

sunflower oil,
for brushing

salt and pepper,
to taste

1 Preheat a grill rack over a campfire
or barbecue.

2 Put the tomato paste, Worcestershire sauce,
garlic, and honey in a plastic bag and mix
together. Season with salt and pepper. Add
the chicken wings and toss to coat evenly
with the sauce.

3 Brush the preheated rack with oil. Place
the chicken wings on the rack and cook
for 10 minutes, turning occasionally. Baste
with any remaining sauce, then cook for an
additional 10–15 minutes, until the chicken
is tender and the juices run clear when
the tip of a sharp knife is inserted into the
thickest part of the meat. Serve the chicken
hot or cold.

Marinate the uncooked, coated
chicken wings in an airtight
plastic container for up to
8 hours in the refrigerator.

MEDITERRANEAN TURKEY BURGERS

 Serves: 4

Prep: 10 mins

Cook: 10 mins

1¼ pounds
ground turkey

2 garlic cloves,
finely chopped

3 tablespoons
drained and chopped
sun-dried tomatoes
(packed in oil)

2 scallions, white and
light green parts only,
thinly sliced

¾ teaspoon salt

½ teaspoon pepper

¾ cup crumbled
feta cheese

To serve

4 seeded burger
buns, halved and
toasted

mayonnaise

1 large tomato, sliced

fresh basil leaves

1 Preheat a grill rack over a campfire
or barbecue.

2 Put all the ingredients into a large bowl
and combine. Form the mixture into
four patties.

3 Place the patties on the preheated rack and
cook for about 5 minutes on each side, or
until cooked through. Serve on the toasted
burger buns with the mayonnaise, tomato
slices, and basil leaves.

For a slightly sweeter flavor,
swap the sun-dried tomatoes
in the burger mix for chopped
roasted red peppers from a jar.

CHEDDAR-JALAPEÑO BURGERS

 Serves: 4

Prep: 10 mins

Cook: 10–15 mins

1½ pounds ground chuck beef

1 extra-large egg, lightly beaten

2 scallions, thinly sliced

1–2 jalapeño chiles, seeded and finely chopped

2 tablespoons finely chopped fresh cilantro

2 tablespoons Worcestershire sauce

1 cup shredded sharp cheddar cheese

salt and pepper, to taste

To serve

4 seeded burger buns, halved and toasted

tomato slices

lettuce

ketchup

1 Preheat a grill rack over a campfire or barbecue. In a large bowl, combine the beef, egg, scallions, chiles, cilantro, Worcestershire sauce, and salt and pepper. Form the mixture into eight equal balls and flatten them into patties about ½ inch thick. Top half of the patties with shredded cheese, leaving a clear border around the edge of each patty.

2 Place the remaining four patties on top of the cheese-topped patties and press the edges together to enclose the cheese. Flatten again into ¾-inch thick patties, making sure that the edges are well sealed.

3 Place on the preheated rack and cook for 5–8 minutes on each side, until done to your liking. Serve on the toasted burger buns with tomato slices, lettuce, and ketchup.

HOT DOGS

Serves: 4

Prep: 10 mins

Cook: 6–8 mins

---

1 red onion

1 tablespoon sunflower oil, for brushing

8 frankfurters

4 hot dog buns

1 cup drained sauerkraut

3 tablespoons Dijon mustard

salt and pepper, to taste

1 Preheat a grill rack over a campfire or barbecue. Cut the onion into thick, round slices, brush with oil, and sprinkle with salt and pepper.

2 Place the onion slices on the preheated rack and cook for 6–8 minutes, turning once, until golden brown. Meanwhile, place the frankfurters on the rack and cook for 4–6 minutes, turning once, until heated through.

3 Slice the buns in half lengthwise and add a spoonful of sauerkraut to each. Place the frankfurters in the buns and sandwich back together. Add a spoonful of mustard and serve immediately with the onions.

Alternatively, cook the frankfurters in a saucepan of boiling water, beef stock, or beer for 5 minutes and serve as above.

PORK SPARERIBS

 Serves: 4

Prep: 15 mins
+ marinating

Cook: 2–2¼hrs

1 rack pork spareribs,
weighing 4–5 pounds

1 onion, peeled and
quartered

2 bay leaves

2 teaspoons whole
black peppercorns

1 teaspoon salt

1 cup barbecue sauce

1. Place the ribs in a large saucepan (cut the rack in half, if necessary) and cover with cold water. Add the onion, bay leaves, peppercorns, and salt and bring to a boil over high heat. Reduce the heat to low and simmer for 1½–2 hours, testing occasionally during the last 30 minutes of cooking. Remove from the heat once the meat begins to pull apart with little resistance. Drain the ribs, discarding the onion, peppercorns, and bay leaves.

2. Coat the ribs with half of the barbecue sauce, then cover and refrigerate for a minimum of 2 hours (and a maximum of 8 hours). Remove from the refrigerator 30 minutes before you are ready to start cooking.

3. Meanwhile, preheat a grill rack over a campfire or barbecue. Baste the ribs with some of the remaining barbecue sauce, place on the preheated grill rack, and cook over high heat for 12–15 minutes on each side, turning and basting every 5–10 minutes, until caramelized and just beginning to blacken in places.

4. Remove from the heat and let stand for 5 minutes. Cut into individual ribs and serve, brushed with any remaining sauce.

SPAGHETTI WITH MEAT SAUCE

 Serves: 4

 Prep: 10 mins

Cook: 40 mins

2 tablespoons
olive oil

1 onion, chopped

1 large green bell
pepper, seeded
and chopped

1 pound ground
round beef

½ cup red wine

2½ cups tomato
puree or tomato
sauce

1 pound dried
spaghetti

salt and pepper,
to taste

1 Heat the oil in a large saucepan over a campfire, stove, or barbecue. Add the onion and green bell pepper and sauté for 3–4 minutes, stirring, until soft.

2 Add the beef and cook for an additional 3–4 minutes, until lightly browned. Add the wine, bring to a boil, and cook until most of the liquid has evaporated. Add the tomato puree or sauce and season with salt and pepper. Bring to a boil, then cover and simmer for 30 minutes, stirring occasionally.

3 Meanwhile, bring a large saucepan of lightly salted water to a boil, then add the spaghetti, bring back to a boil, and cook according to the package directions, until tender but still firm to the bite. Drain well and divide among four serving bowls.

4 Spoon the sauce over the spaghetti and serve immediately.

24

A long, slow simmer will give you tender, tasty meat—if the sauce dries out, add beef stock or water as necessary.

TUNA STEAKS
(with chile & ginger marinade)

Serves: 4

Prep: 10 mins
+ marinating

Cook: 12–15 mins

4 tuna steaks, ¾ inch thick, weighing 6 ounces each

2 tablespoons olive oil, plus extra for greasing

salt and pepper, to taste

lime wedges, to serve

Chile & ginger marinade

½ cup firmly packed brown sugar

½ cup water

1-inch piece fresh ginger, thinly shredded

1 Thai chile or jalapeño chile, seeded and finely chopped

1 large garlic clove, crushed

juice of ½ lime

1   To make the marinade, put the sugar and water in a small saucepan and bring to a boil. Boil for 7–8 minutes, until syrupy. Add the ginger, chile, garlic, and lime juice, and boil for another minute. Pour into a bowl and let cool completely.

2   Put the tuna steaks in a single layer in a shallow dish. Brush on both sides with the oil and rub with salt and pepper to taste. Pour the cold marinade over the tuna steaks, turning to coat. Cover with plastic wrap and let marinate in the refrigerator for 30–40 minutes, turning occasionally.

3   Preheat a grill rack over a campfire or barbecue. Place the tuna steaks in a hinged wire grill basket, reserving the marinade. Place the basket on the preheated grill rack and cook for 2 minutes. Turn and cook the other side for 1 minute. Remove from the basket and wrap in aluminum foil to keep warm.

4   Pour the reserved marinade into a small saucepan. Bring to a boil and boil for 2 minutes. Pour into a small bowl. Arrange the tuna on serving plates and serve immediately with lime wedges and the hot marinade.

BAD WEATHER BLUES
(AND HOW TO BEAT THEM...)

People can be pretty resourceful when it comes to dealing with the weather and its unpredictability. But when you're camping and the weather is bad, sometimes some forward planning can make all the difference. Here are a few ideas on how to overcome those bad weather blues.

Do your research—before you leave, do some research on the local area, including places of interest nearby, days out, and indoor events. Print out what you can and bring it along so that you have some ideas on hand for filling rainy days.

Pack some board games—the oldies are the best and you can't go wrong with a simple deck of cards. Fun, competitive play is a great way to pass the day.

Bring an extra groundsheet. It will be a great asset in wet weather, allowing you to create a designated space in the tent for muddy boots, and helping you to keep damp and dirt out of your sleeping compartments.

Keep extras—have a pair of clean, dry socks and a change of clothes in your pack. Once wet, it's difficult to get an outfit dry again in the great outdoors, and staying warm and dry is a must

Head to the coffee shop! If all else fails, head to a local coffee shop, diner, or even a restaurant— a nice hot drink makes a great pick-me-up on a miserable day.

Prepare for a night in—if it's really raining cats and dogs, batten down the hatches. Tighten the guy ropes, pull your things away from the sides of the tent, and cozy up—you might just have to wait it out!

LEMON-STEAMED SALMON

Serves: 4

Prep: 5 mins

Cook: 15 mins

4 salmon fillets

1 lemon

4 tablespoons butter

salt and pepper, to taste

1 Preheat a grill rack over a campfire or barbecue. Cut four 12-inch squares of double-thickness aluminum foil. Place a piece of salmon on each square and sprinkle with salt and pepper. Cut four slices from the lemon and place a slice on top of each piece of salmon. Top with a pat of butter and squeeze the juice from the remaining lemon over the fish.

2 Loosely wrap the salmon in the foil, sealing firmly with the seam on top. Place the packages on the preheated grill rack and cook for about 15 minutes, or until the fish flakes easily when tested with a fork.

3 Open the packages and serve the fish in the lemon butter juices.

Try spreading 2 tablespoons of store-bought green pesto on the salmon (in place of the lemon slices and juice).

LOADED CAMPFIRE POTATOES

Serves: 4

Prep: 15 mins

Cook: 1–1¼ hrs

olive oil, for brushing

4 large baking potatoes

1 cup shredded cheddar cheese

salt and pepper, to taste

Broccoli filling

1½ cups small broccoli florets

2 tablespoons butter

Bacon & sour cream filling

2 bacon slices, chopped

¼ cup sour cream

1 Brush four 12-inch squares of double-thickness aluminum foil with oil. Prick the potatoes with a fork, then tightly wrap each in a foil square. Place in the hot coals around the edge of a campfire or barbecue and cook for about 1 hour, turning occasionally, until tender.

2 To make the broccoli filling, place the broccoli on a large square of double-thickness foil, then top with the butter and season with salt and pepper. Gather up the edges of the foil loosely and fold over at the top to seal. Add to the hot coals about 20 minutes before the potatoes are cooked.

3 To make the bacon and sour cream filling, put the bacon in a skillet over high heat and cook in its own fat, stirring, until crisp and golden. Mix the sour cream with the bacon.

4 Once cooked, cut the potatoes in half, scoop out the flesh, and mash with a fork. Reserve the foil squares. Stir in your chosen filling ingredients (broccoli or bacon and sour cream), season with salt and pepper, and spoon back into the skins.

5 Sprinkle with the shredded cheese and put the potatoes on the open pieces of foil. Place around the edge of the fire for 2–3 minutes, until the cheese is melted, then serve.

For extra cheesy potato skins, add an extra 1 cup shredded cheddar cheese along with your chosen filling ingredients.

CAMPFIRE FRIES

Serves: 4

Prep: 10 mins

Cook: 10–12 mins

olive oil, for pan-frying (enough to coat the fries)

2 medium sweet potatoes, peeled and cut into thin sticks

2 teaspoons steak seasoning (or Cajun spice mix)

salt, to taste

mayonnaise, to serve

1 Heat the oil in a nonstick skillet over a campfire, stove, or barbecue.

2 Add the sweet potatoes, sprinkle with the steak seasoning, and toss well. Gently cook for about 10–12 minutes, turning regularly, until the fries are just tender. Sprinkle with salt and serve with mayonnaise.

GARLIC BREAD

Serves: 6

Prep: 5 mins

Cook: 10–15 mins

1¼ sticks butter, softened

3 garlic cloves, crushed

2 tablespoons chopped fresh parsley

pepper, to taste

1 large or 2 small French bread loaves

1 Preheat a grill rack over a campfire or barbecue. Mix together the butter, garlic, and parsley in a bowl until well combined. Season with pepper and mix well.

2 Make several lengthwise cuts in the bread, being careful not to cut all the way through.

3 Spread the flavored butter over one side of each cut and place the loaf on a large sheet of aluminum foil.

4 Wrap up the bread in the foil and cook on the preheated grill rack for 10–15 minutes, until the butter melts and the bread is piping hot.

GRILLED FIG & BLUE CHEESE SANDWICHES

(with radicchio & balsamic-glazed onions)

Serves: 4

Prep: 10 mins

Cook: 40–50 mins

---

12 large figs, stems removed

8 ounces blue cheese

4 cheese-topped rolls, halved and toasted

1 small head radicchio, cut into julienne strips

Balsamic-glazed onions

2 tablespoons olive oil

2 red onions, thinly sliced

½ teaspoon salt

2 tablespoons balsamic vinegar

1 To make the balsamic-glazed onions, heat the oil in a large, heavy skillet over a campfire, stove, or barbecue. Add the onions, reduce the heat to medium, and cook, stirring occasionally, for 10 minutes. Stir in the salt and continue to cook for an additional 20–30 minutes, stirring frequently, until the onions are soft and browned. Stir in the vinegar and cook, stirring, for another minute to deglaze the pan. Remove from the heat and set aside.

2 If using wooden skewers, soak one per person in cold water for 30 minutes prior to cooking to prevent them from burning.

3 Preheat a grill rack over a campfire or barbecue. Thread the figs onto the presoaked wooden skewers or metal skewers and place on the preheated grill rack. Cook over medium heat for about 10 minutes, turning every few minutes, until the skins are just beginning to blacken. Remove from the heat and halve lengthwise.

4 Spread the cheese on the bottom halves of the toasted rolls. Top each with a few spoonfuls of the balsamic onions, a couple of handfuls of the radicchio, and six fig halves. Place the other half of the roll on top. Serve immediately.

BLACK BEAN BURGERS

 Serves: 4

Prep: 20 mins

Cook: 20 mins

½ cup bulgur wheat

⅔ cup boiling water

1 (15-ounce) can black beans, drained and rinsed

2 tablespoons finely chopped onion

1 extra-large egg

1 cup plain dry bread crumbs

¼ cup barbecue sauce, plus extra to serve

1 teaspoon salt

½ teaspoon pepper

To serve

4 burger buns, halved and toasted

tomato slices

lettuce leaves

1 Put the bulgur wheat into a bowl, pour the boiling water over the grains, and set aside for 15 minutes. Pour off any excess water.

2 In a food processor, combine half the beans with the onion, egg, bread crumbs, barbecue sauce, salt, and pepper, and process until smooth. Put the remaining beans into a bowl and mash with a fork, leaving them a little chunky. Stir the processed bean mixture into the mashed beans, together with the soaked and drained bulgur wheat. Form the mixture into four patties, cover, and chill in the refrigerator until ready to cook.

3 Preheat a grill rack over a campfire or barbecue. Place the patties on the preheated grill rack and cook over high heat for about 8–10 minutes on each side, until brown and beginning to get crisp on the outside. Serve on the toasted burger buns with additional barbecue sauce, tomato slices, and lettuce.

Prepare the black bean mixture and shape into patties at home, then keep refrigerated until needed.

HOT CHOCOLATE

 Serves: 2

 Prep: 5 mins

Cook: 10 mins

---

2 ounces semisweet chocolate, broken into pieces, plus extra to decorate

1¼ cups milk

1 Place the chocolate in a saucepan. Pour the milk into another saucepan and heat over a campfire, stove, or barbecue until it is just simmering. Pour about one-quarter of the milk onto the chocolate and let stand until the chocolate has softened.

2 Beat the milk-and-chocolate mixture until smooth. Return the remaining milk to the heat and simmer, then pour onto the chocolate mixture, whisking continuously.

3 Pour into mugs and decorate with extra pieces of chocolate. Serve immediately.

Swap half of the milk for cream and decorate with miniature marshmallows for a decadent drink!

POPCORN
(with maple syrup butter)

 Serves: 4

 Prep: 5 mins

Cook: 5 mins

1–2 tablespoons vegetable oil

⅔ cup popping corn

1 tablespoon butter

3 tablespoons maple syrup

1 tablespoon sesame seeds (optional)

1. Heat the oil in a nonstick saucepan over a campfire, stove, or barbecue.

2. Carefully add the popping corn to the pan in an even layer and cover with a lid.

3. Cook the popping corn over gentle heat, shaking the pan occasionally, until the corn kernels pop.

4. Pour the popcorn into a large mixing bowl, discarding any kernels that have not popped.

5. Melt the butter in a small saucepan, then pour in the maple syrup. Bring to a boil, then remove from the heat and cool. Pour the maple syrup sauce over the popcorn and add the sesame seeds, if using. Serve immediately.

Drizzle with melted chocolate or caramelized sugar as an alternative to maple syrup butter.

DOUBLE CHOC CHIP S'MORES

 Serves: **4**

 Prep: **5 mins**

Cook: **2–3 mins**

- - - - - - - - - - - - - - - -

8 small squares milk chocolate

8 chocolate chip cookies

12 white marshmallows

1 If using wooden skewers, soak one per person in cold water for 30 minutes prior to cooking to prevent them from burning. Place two squares of chocolate on four of the cookies.

2 Thread the marshmallows onto the presoaked wooden skewers or metal skewers and toast over a campfire, stove, or barbecue for about 1 minute, turning, until starting to melt and turn brown.

3 Quickly press the marshmallows onto the chocolate-topped cookies and place another cookie on top of each, pressing lightly so that you can pull out the skewers. Serve immediately.

For traditional all-American s'mores, use graham crackers instead of the chocolate chip cookies.

FRUIT SKEWERS
(with chocolate sauce)

Serves: 4

Prep: 10 mins

Cook: 10 mins

a selection of fresh fruit, such as apricots, peaches, strawberries, mangoes, pineapple, and bananas, prepared and cut into chunks

maple syrup, for brushing

2 ounces semisweet chocolate, broken into chunks

2 tablespoons heavy cream

1 If using wooden skewers, soak one per person in cold water for 30 minutes prior to cooking to prevent them from burning.

2 Thread alternate pieces of fruit onto the presoaked wooden skewers or metal skewers. Brush the fruit with a little maple syrup.

3 Put the chocolate in a heatproof bowl, set the bowl over a saucepan of barely simmering water, and heat over a campfire, stove, or barbecue, until the chocolate has melted. Add the cream and beat until smooth.

4 Meanwhile, cook the fruit skewers over the campfire or barbecue for 3 minutes, or until caramelized. Serve with the chocolate sauce.

The natural sugars in the fruit will caramelize over the heat, creating a delicious sweet, crisp glaze.